AQUARIUS HOROSCOPE & ASTROLOGY 2020

Aquarius Horoscope & Astrology 2020

Copyright © 2019

Mystic Shores Publishing house

Published by Mystic Shores publications

Suite SM-2380-6403

14601 North Bybee Lake Court

Portland, Oregon 97203

Phone: +1 (805) 308-6503

islandauthor@hotmail.com

Copyright © 2019 by Mystic Shores publications

All rights reserved. This book or any portion thereof may not be reproduced or used in any manner whatsoever without the express written permission of the publisher except for the use of brief quotations in a book review.

The information accessible from this book is for informational purposes only. None of the data within should be regarded as a promise of benefits, a statutory warranty, or a guarantee of results to be achieved.

Images are used under license from Fotosearch & Dreamstime.

Acknowledgment:

*Thank you to the stargazers, dreamers, and mystics.
You make this world a better place.*

AQUARIUS 2020 OVERVIEW

2020 is an incredible year for Aquarius. Inspiration fans the ideas which sail into Aquarius's life, this encourages new ideas and concepts which inspire growth. Not one, not two, not three, but four Supermoons in 2020 ensures plenty of fantastic energy arrives to inspire Aquarius to develop innovative dreams in tune with their wildest ideas and aspirations. There is astonishing progress to be made towards by following your heart in 2020, Aquarius utilizes the power of air to make progress on their most ambitious dreams.

Mercury Retrograde is the most significant destabilizing force in 2020. Forewarned is forearmed and Aquarius does find that bridges can be burnt if not handled sensitively. Being careful with interpersonal relationships allows Aquarius to navigate a delicate path through these troublesome cosmic storms. Aquarius can harness the air power of their mind and spirit to find solutions and take an affirmative action before relationships veer off course.

2020 is a year which blends the elemental forces of Earth, Air, Fire, and Water with new world technology. This dramatically expands your star signs creative abilities. The star sign Aquarius is one of air dominance, and when harnessed correctly, you make remarkable progress as they light the path forward with their burning desires. Inspiration and idealistic ventures abound for Aquarius in this most incredible year of potentiality.

With so many compelling reasons to shine, the star sign Aquarius can look forward to incredible cosmic energy, which helps increase and boost their potential possible in 2020, and beyond.

Aquarius

Aquarius Dates: January 20 to February 18
Symbol: Water Bearer
Element: Air
Planets: Saturn, Uranus
House: Eleventh
Colors: Silver, blue

JANUARY ASTROLOGY

January 3 – First Quarter Moon in Aries.

This Moon phase occurs at 04.45 UTC.

January 3, 4 - Quadrantids Meteor Shower.

The Quadrantids meteor shower run yearly from January 1-5. The Quadrantids meteor shower peaks this year on the night of the 3rd and morning of the 4th.

January 10 - Full Moon in Cancer.

This full moon phase occurs at 19:21 UTC. This full moon is called the Full Wolf Moon because this was the time of year when hungry wolf packs howled outside camps. This full moon has also been known as the Old Moon and the Moon After Yule.

January 10 - Penumbral Lunar Eclipse.

A penumbral lunar eclipse occurs as the Moon passes through the Earth's partial shadow or penumbra. During this type of eclipse, the Moon will darken slightly but won't wholly eclipse. This penumbral eclipse is visible throughout most of Europe, Africa, Asia, and Western Australia.

January 17 – Last Quarter Moon in Libra.

This Moon phase occurs at 12.58 UTC.

January 24 – New Moon in Capricorn.

This new moon phase occurs at 21:42 UTC. The Moon is on the same side of the Earth as the Sun and will not be visible in the night sky. This phase occurs at 21:03 UTC. This is an excellent time to view galaxies and stars as there is no moonlight to obscure your view of the universe.

JANUARY HOROSCOPE

JANUARY WEEK ONE

There are lots to look forward to in the chapter ahead, it does link to new options which inspire your mind. It enables you to do your best, you discover the open road with fascinating areas to explore. This brings the unexpected potential for you to contemplate, it is an active and lively chapter where you can expand your horizons and take in a refreshing vista of potentiality. The area you nurture is the one which grows and blossoms. A new role for you which is linked to your current position. This elevates your status and provides you with ample security, it does show restructuring is taking place and that can feel unsettling, keep focusing on producing stellar results, a highly productive chapter is coming, which enables you to plot a course towards the achievement of your goals. A sense of recognition for a job well done is here soon. Possibilities are arriving, which gives you a strong sense of presence, it lights up a path of great joy, and this inspires your mind with fascinating options to explore. It is a boost your confidence as you do feel encouraged to push back barriers, and reach for something more that becomes a passion project.

Furthermore, there is a sweet surprise arriving for you soon. It does lead to an inspirational chapter where you can explore an area which is unique and special. It is a lively chapter where your social life holds the key to expansion. It does see a great deal of activity going on, with so much happening, you are sure to make the most of this enriching phase.

JANUARY WEEK TWO

This is a time where you can contemplate the options ahead, and plot a course towards achieving a positive outcome. Long-term goals are highlighted as coming into focus, and this provides you with essential planning that helps you address strategy and manageability. Highlighting a path to does provide you with a focused trajectory, a substantial result soon follows. This brings a fair offer to your table. This is a time which favors expansion, it sees you stepping out and exploring the possibilities available. A new venture arrives to brighten your life, it does initiate a chapter which looks promising. This week also speaks of a welcome surprise coming, this relates to your social life, all indications point to the beginning of a new chapter for you.

Whatever comes or goes, you are entering a cycle of change. This supports personal growth on all levels, it brings information to light, which you can no longer deny or hide. It has you questioning the path ahead, and wanting to go in a direction which is in alignment with your true feelings. It may be that a new friendship ignites soon, and this provides you with a rich source of inspiration and joy. The past is a prism into the person you are today, it has deepened your emotional awareness, and does give you beautiful memories to contemplate. Currently, you are at a loose end, and this restless vibe is encouraging you to begin an exciting new chapter. The outlook is far brighter than you realize, you are moving towards an abundant episode which rules expansion and harmony. An offer makes its way known to you soon.

JANUARY WEEK THREE

This week is all about someone in your life, this person is in your social circle, and you most likely have a good idea about who I am talking about. The reason is that this person has captured your interest, there is a strong indication that this is a situation that is worth exploring further. There is communication likely to reach you soon, this sets the stage for a lively chapter ahead. You have dealt with the past adequately, you can let that chapter go, this lights up a new vision to explore. It does lead to a highly productive section where you can reach for impressive results. An encounter arrives, which sparks your interest, it does show a person with old-fashioned values, who seeks to develop a meaningful bond with you. It shows you linked with this person in the most harmonious way. You are entering a golden phase, which brings good fortune and luck to your situation. It's a time where you are magnetic and charismatic, circulating in social environments does bring benefits to your door. There is a theme emerging which relates to opportunities to mingle, and generally, you can expect to have more activity occurring in your social life soon. It does put you in the mood to mingle, networking with other characters opens the pathway to a more abundant chapter. It does indicate that these discussions help initiate a new venture for you soon. Harnessing the power of an abundant mindset is going to lead to a change of fortune, it does create instant change, it sets the tone for positivity to quickly boost your situation. It does have you feeling different, you no longer are drawn into toxic environments that bring your energy downward. It is a valuable tool that becomes more powerful, the more you utilize it. It brings your situation to a more productive and stronger chapter.

JANUARY WEEK FOUR

You're ready to craft your vision into a journey towards advancing a goal of yours. As you focus on increasing the abundance in your world, you mark a significant turning point, which sees potential skyrocket. It does culminate in achieving a substantial phase of growth, and this, in essence, creates a gateway to a new level of performance. It is your time to shine. There is a theme of good fortune and luck emerging in your world soon. It does have you feeling light-hearted, and this sees you stepping out towards expanding your horizons. It leads to a busy and productive phase, which puts a strong focus on achieving goals. This sets the stage for a prosperous passage towards elevating your situation. You radiate a vibrancy which does raise the potential in your world. These positive influences heighten your ability to manifest your goals, you reveal exceptional potential, which leads you towards a direction which is in alignment with your personal vision. It does have you focusing on achieving a stellar result. It is a time of inspired possibilities which leave you feeling optimistic about the future. You are given the green light to connect with your creativity and shift towards expanding your goals. Harnessing the power of manifestation is at the crux of this incredible chapter. There is a strong sense of abundance emerging, which helps you achieve your goals with surprising accuracy. You discover a path which beckons to be developed, your curious mind is delighted with the potential possible. Things begin to come together nicely for you. Something you dearly wanted suddenly materializes, this leads to a chapter of excitement and adventure.

FEBRUARY ASTROLOGY

February 2 – First Quarter Moon in Taurus. This Moon phase occurs at 1.42 UTC.

February 9 - Full Moon in Leo, Supermoon.

The Moon is on the opposite side of the Earth as the Sun and will be fully illuminated. This phase occurs at 7:33 UTC. This full moon is known as the Full Snow Moon because the heaviest snows usually fall during this month. Since hunting is difficult, this full moon has also been recognized as the Full Hunger Moon, since the harsh weather made fishing difficult. This is the first of four supermoons for 2020. The Moon will be at its nearest approach to the Earth and will look slightly larger and brighter than usual.

February 10 - Mercury at largest Eastern Elongation.

The planet Mercury reaches an eastern elongation of 18.1 degrees from the Sun.

February 15 – Last Quarter Moon in Scorpio.

This Moon phase occurs at 22.17 UTC.

February 18 – Mercury Retrograde begins in Pisces.

During a retrograde period, it isn't the right time to move forward in any practical venture. Be prepared for misunderstandings and miscommunications to be prevalent.

February 23 - New Moon in Aquarius.

The Moon is on the same side of the Earth as the Sun and will not be visible in the night sky. This phase occurs at 15:32 UTC. This is an excellent time to view galaxies and stars as there is no moonlight to obscure your view of the universe.

FEBRUARY HOROSCOPE

FEBRUARY WEEK ONE

There are some excellent potential brewing in your life. It leads to an expansive chapter which draws harmony into your world, and this has you thinking creatively about nurturing a pet project. It does lead to a happy section where you become involved in areas which spike your interest, and you become more involved spending time in a social setting. This is the time which offers you room to improve your situation. It does help you channel a powerful message that things are on the mend in your life. If you have felt, emotionally blocked, this is set to resolve. It helps you open your mind and heart to new opportunities, it brings confidence into your world and encourages you to expand your horizons. This is a time of expansion for you, it takes you towards new adventures, happy experiences, and creative expression. Don't hold back, enjoy yourself in a new area, unleashing your potential, leads to a leap of faith. Perhaps you can develop a venture which has been on the back burner for some time. It's an ideal time to take a stellar leap into the potential possible. It's a perfect time to link up with new potential, you are ready to create space for some new adventures. It does let you put into play a practical action plan which enables your big ideas to hold water. This leads to an active chapter, it allows you to accomplish your larger goals. It could lead to a fresh start on many levels.

FEBRUARY WEEK TWO

The February 9th Supermoon flows a river of heightened potential into your sphere. Some exciting changes are coming into your life soon. There are lovely changes ahead for you, it sees you working on a dream that is close to your heart, this vision encapsulates your hopes and wishes for the future. It does show that this vision holds promise, you can dream big and get back in sync with where you hope to be. It is a time which highlights abundance flowing into your personal life; finally, you have a path open with blue skies ahead. You discover you can plot a course which has you feeling enthusiastic and inspired about the progress you're able to create. It helps you manifest a situation which is in alignment with where you are hoping to go. Unexpected information crosses your path, which leads to an exciting chapter of developing a substantial goal, it gives you experience in an entirely new area, which is very exciting. Being in this unique setting brings added benefits to your spirit. It is a lively and refreshing chapter, a new beginning heralds the start of enticing energy which flows into your world, it brings with it a character who is insightful, endearing, and enigmatic. Your curious mind seeks to know this person better, opportunities arrive to support this growth, and you soon dive into deep conversations which have you thinking about future prospects. It is a time of adventure and expansion.

FEBRUARY WEEK THREE

New conditions arrive in the workplace, this creates an environment which is shifting, it's more relevant and suitable with your current goals, it does reflect a productive chapter, one where you may find yourself tested, but you have the skills to make the most of this active phase. You sail through towards a role which offers you room to expand and grow your situation. Security is at the basis of this vital energy. A secret will be revealed soon, this news has you finding out more about a person who has been acting mysteriously recently. If you feel that you are being undermined, announcing this news will help bring everything out in the open, this enables you to create an environment which is more grounded, and even. It does release outworn energy and paves the way for a new chapter with this character. You head towards a path which emphasizes fresh beginnings, clarity, and insight provide you with some stellar ideas to explore. It does have you in the mood to expand your social circle, communication soon supports this endeavor. Invitations to mingle provide you with ample option to strut your stuff in a more active phase of networking with others who you connect well with. You discover a slow burn friendship begins to take off. There is an emphasis on dealing with issues that have held back progress, you may find the situation crops up, which needs tackling to move forward. It does suggest that this draws harmony into your life, it enables you to plot a course towards future growth.

FEBRUARY WEEK FOUR

Change is coming, this is positive, it has you thinking about the potential possible. Paying attention to your goals does open a door towards an area which is worth investigating. It is a time of adventure, you explore your options, and discover a path which offers a bevy of exciting possibilities. It brings happiness and can lead to impressive results. Concentrating on achieving those bigger personal goals does set the right intention, it is helpful as it sends out a message that you are ready to expand your horizons and create space for someone new to enter into your life. A breakthrough occurs, this gives you options to explore, it is a time where you can expand your consciousness and embrace a chapter of fun and adventure. This sees a bond forming with one who enriches your life. You are ready to grow and draw new energy into your world. It does lead to a lively chapter where you expand your social circle, new friendships blossom, there is one in particular, which enriches your life, and has you thinking about the potential possible. There is something around the corner, you enter a phase which is ripe for expansion, it helps you initiate significant moves forward, your priorities shift, and it is a time where you draw people into your life. This nourishes your spirit, and you discover one who has an essential role in your future world, this marks a momentous time of developing a situation which holds water, one which can progress further.

MARCH ASTROLOGY

March 2 – First Quarter Moon in Gemini.

This Moon phase occurs at 19.57 UTC.

March 9 - Full Moon in Virgo, Supermoon.

This full Moon phase occurs at 17:48 UTC. This full moon is known as the Full Worm Moon because this was the time of year when the ground would soften, and earthworms would reappear. This full moon is also known as the Full Crow Moon, the Full Crust Moon, the Full Sap Moon, and the Lenten Moon. This is also the last of four super-moons for 2020. The Moon will be closer to the Earth and will look slightly larger and brighter than usual.

March 9 - Mercury Retrograde ends in Aquarius.

You can now move forward with any delayed plans that you have been putting off due to the Mercury Retrograde phase. Relationships should soon improve as miscommunications are overcome

March 16 – Last Quarter Moon in Sagittarius.

This Moon phase occurs at 9.34 UTC. –

March 20 - March Equinox.

The March equinox takes place at 3:50 UTC. The Sun be shining on the equator, and there will be equal amounts of day and night throughout the world. This is the first day of spring (vernal equinox) in the Northern Hemisphere.

March 24 - New Moon in Aries.

The Moon is on the same side of the Earth as the Sun and will not be visible in the night sky. This phase occurs at 9:28 UTC. This is an excellent time to observe galaxies and stars because there is no moonlight to interfere.

March 24 - Mercury at most substantial Western Elongation.

The planet Mercury reaches its most substantial western elongation of 27.8 degrees from the Sun.

March 24 - Venus at most substantial Eastern Elongation.

The planet Venus reaches its most substantial Eastern elongation of 46.1 degrees from the Sun.

MARCH HOROSCOPE

MARCH WEEK ONE

This is an ideal time to ground yourself in a functional area which offers room for growth. You have been through an unpredictable chapter and can now harness the power of rejuvenation to provide you with enticing options to explore. It does create a positive ripple effect which enables refreshing potential to flow into your world soon. The path ahead is ripe with exploration, adventure, and experimenting with new areas. It can feel exciting and exhausting in equal doses. If you have been dreaming about changing career paths, now is the perfect time to seek out new areas to develop. This shifts you towards a journey which offers room to grow your talents, it does have you investing your energy in a functional space which draws abundance into your life. It is best to keep your options open, there are some doubts around you, and this is your intuition guiding you to stay open to a situation which is more conducive to achieving your personal goals. Either this person steps up and becomes more in tune with your direction, or you are going to set the bar high, and keep exploring the new potential available. There is a happy outcome ahead for you. A surprise invitation takes you to an event where you cross the path of a person who captures your interest. This is a big deal, it is a dramatic sign that wakes you up and makes you realize there is potential to create change, which better suits your circumstances. Being open and looking to achieve your personal goals does help you sync up with excitement. This leads to a time of forging new goals with another.

MARCH WEEK TWO

This is the time to dial down the workload and rejuvenate. You will have options to develop your ambitions later in the year. This is a process of taking time to slow down, reflect on your dreams and goals, and spend time with your friends. Reconnecting with your social circle does provide you with emotional sustenance, it allows you to renew your spirit. Recent events may have had you in a backspin, you are currently in a chapter of healing and renewal. Nurturing yourself is important at this time, turning inwards, you create a sanctuary which now enables you to work through any complicated feelings you may be having at this time. It also lights up your imagination as you have time to focus on solutions and ideas. You are entering a chapter which is ruled by compassion and creativity, it reveals areas which need working on, and it does help you ascertain a clearer picture of the potential possible in your personal life. It gives you a chance to delve into future planning, and this leads to beautiful advancement in your world. You soon get the go-ahead to develop a creative idea you've had on the backburner for a while. If you have had a dream blocked, persevering is set to open new pathways for growth. A surge of potential enables a transit towards a chapter paved with advancement. This sees a spike in your enthusiasm, and it does land you in an area which offers room to grow your ideas.

MARCH WEEK THREE

This is a time which underscores powerful healing arriving to help cleanse your spirit and resolve any issues which have held your progress back. You have taken on an energetic burden, and this influence can be released by doing the right mind-body-spirit work. It all leads to a chapter which offers an ideal time of new energy arriving to bring abundance into your world. You are in a time where you can feel sentimental, it is a great time which draws healing into your world. A lunar eclipse combines with a full moon blessing this week. This is why you may be feeling emotionally sensitive, and restless., It is a great time to nurture your spirit and take a moment to reflect on the abundance in your world. Life may have thrown you a curveball recently, but there is a larger plan emerging, which relates to beginning a chapter which offers you room to grow your life, it enables you to head towards a more abundant future. Your resilience and tenacity support your efforts, you draw strength into your spirit. It does provide you with significant options to explore, a shift is coming soon, this opens a gateway for future growth. Change is coming, which enables you to strike a balance between progress and stability. It can feel awkward to reach for something major, taking time to plot your course will provide you with a path which is structured, and this becomes a stepping stone towards the type of growth you are seeking. You brew some excellent possibilities soon. You touch down on a new area which offers you room to grow your goals. It may help to map out a step-by-step plan to achieve this type of advancement. It is an auspicious time to develop your skills and learn an area which offers room for progression. It is a path which lights sparks of inspiration, and it does get you involved in forging ahead towards the realization of your dreams.

MARCH WEEK FOUR

If you have found the road ahead was blocked, you can use this time to gain insight into how to create an increase of potential. Doing your due diligence puts enables you to spot the potential in an area which crosses your path soon. It does charge up your creative aspect and leads to an insightful time where you can reinvent your life, and draw new potential. You scope out a new area soon. Developing this path could lead to a reinvention, which improves your situation on many levels. It puts the spotlight on a fresh and exciting dynamic, and this has you feeling creative and inspired. It does see structure coming, which enables you to apply focused intention to achieve robust growth. Your talents are superb, it helps you reach great heights of excellence when you put your energy into something. Your expertise will hold you in good stead. Soon, a sense of recognition arrives, and you feel proud of being able to make a difference. This is an ideal time to look for a new assignment which captures your interest. Your creativity is on the rise, artistic expression may well be the ticket to expanding your horizons, it could lead to progress, which improves your bottom line. An outlet for your creativity does offer a path which draws advancement into your life. It does deliver new friendships, and this brings harmony into your world. It is a time of harnessing your imagination to good effect. You make progress on an area which is a priority, developing your goals leads to a path opening. Traveling in this direction reflects a desire to improve your situation, you are willing to work and do what is necessary to open a gateway towards a brighter future. Your life brims with quality options over the coming chapter, it has you feeling inspired about the advancement possible.

APRIL ASTROLOGY

April 1 – First Quarter Moon in Cancer.

This Moon phase occurs at 10.21 UTC.

April 8 - Full Moon in Libra, Supermoon.

The Moon is on the opposite side of the Earth as the Sun and will be completely illuminated. This moon phase occurs at 2:35 UTC. This full moon is known as Full Pink Moon because it marked an appearance of the first spring flowers. This full moon has also been identified as the Sprouting Grass Moon, the Growing Moon, and the Egg Moon. Many coastal areas call it Full Fish Moon because this was the time the fish swam upriver to breed.

April 14 – Last Quarter Moon in Capricorn.

This Moon phase occurs at 22.56 UTC.

April 22, 23 - Lyrids Meteor Shower.

The Lyrids meteor shower runs each year from April 16-25. This meteor shower peaks on the night of the 22nd and the morning of the 23rd. These meteors sometimes produce blazing dust trails that last for several seconds.

April 23 - New Moon in Taurus.

The New Moon is on the same side of the Earth as the Sun and will not be visible in the night sky. This moon phase occurs at 2:26 UTC. This is an excellent time to observe galaxies and stars because there is no moonlight visible.

April 30 – First Quarter Moon in Leo.

This Moon phase occurs at 20.38 UTC.

APRIL HOROSCOPE

APRIL WEEK ONE

Someone from the past reaches out to share the important news with you. It does take you to an exciting phase where you share discussions and ideas with someone who holds meaning to you. Developing a closer bond with this person bolsters your mood, it shuffles the decks of potential and draws a meaningful connection into your life. Your best qualities shine, it does highlight a time of abundance and inspiration ahead. It is a time of nervous energy, as you focus on the chapter ahead, you may discover you feel restless, excited, and tense all at once. However, there is a scene forward, which is characterized by the relaxed ambiance and natural tranquillity, great success, fulfillment, and abundance are ahead. There are many enticing options to explore, you are headed towards a time which reinvigorates your spirit, and nurtures a meaningful bond. This week speaks of unexpected news arriving, this information comes out of the blue, it provides you with an opportunity to grow your situation and achieve an important goal you have had on the back burner for a while now. As you approach this situation, do your due diligence to make sure it ticks all the boxes for you. It does see you achieve a fresh start in a new area.

APRIL WEEK TWO

You may need to set boundaries and spend time contemplating the path ahead. Clarifying your priorities does help you navigate towards a brighter future. You are undergoing a transition which shifts your energy forward. This can feel unsettling, as change takes you out of your comfort zone. However, there are new adventures to take in which inspire and delight.

Further information is coming, which will help clarify the situation you're in, this leads to you been able to decide what to do next. It does help improve your condition and brings you to a stage where you feel that things have dramatically shifted to a better place. Taking an active role does lead to positive change. You may feel undervalued in the workplace, this is difficult, as you are taken for granted, and it does make it difficult to progress and advance your situation. However, there is new energy coming, this provides fresh inspiration and creative ideas to further your options in the workplace. You may discover a phase of essential growth comes out of this chapter, this leads to expansion, which heightens your sense of security. Any turbulence you are experiencing in your career at this time is resolved, you discover an area to head towards, it does enable you to get a plan into action, this provides you with a beautiful journey of growth. It's a busy time where your job description could change, and you are okay with exploring a fresh start. Progress soon follows as doors are opening for you in the workplace.

APRIL WEEK THREE

You are set to enter an optimistic chapter, it offers you options to circulate, this social growth does inspire a light-hearted environment. It has you spending time with friends and family. This lights your life with rejuvenating and refreshing energy. It is an ideal time to expand your dreams and push back barriers which have limited progress in your life. This is a lovely time to contemplate your goals, you may feel a need to change your priorities and bring a new element into your life. It does show that reshuffling your options can bring a fantastic opportunity to your door. A vision takes shape, taking time to examine the potential possible will give you a better picture of the growth likely before you make a firm decision. Your future does take you to a path which advances your goals, it leads you on a journey of grace and sophistication, this elevates your situation and enables you to mingle with characters that share a similar journey. It does open a new path, a new chapter awaits your open heart, this is a time which is all about fresh beginnings, new opportunities, and positive outcomes, which light a path forward for you.

APRIL WEEK FOUR

New options flowing into your world soon. It does have you exploring a business-minded venture, it could see you score a significant lifestyle change, this brings you towards a phase where you harness the power of your determination, and make a strong and courageous pitch towards achieving an important goal. This lines up beautifully with your aspirations, things begin to fall into place for you. You are doing the right thing by expanding your horizons. In fact, an opportunity arrives soon, which offers you a sense of abundance. It leads to a chapter of growth, which is self-expressive, creative, and idealistic. It leads to a time of inspiration as you enjoy developing a project, close your heart. It's a motivating time which is filled with refreshing ideas and concepts. You're likely to see some change occurring in your life soon, this draws creative elements, and it does fire your instincts to help you intuitively discern the right area to develop. This type of change is suitable, it is essential for your continued evolution, and does open, refreshing options which help progress your life, it beautifully orients your energy forward. It is a time which offers you hope, it is a time where you can align your spirit forward, you discover an area that speaks to your heart. It does provide you an angle towards a more abundant future. As you progress your situation, you feel blessed to have followed your intuition.

MAY ASTROLOGY

May 6, 7 - Eta Aquarids Meteor Shower.

The Eta Aquarids meteor shower runs annually from April 19 to May 28. It peaks this year on the night of May 6 and the morning of May 7.

May 7 - Full Moon in Scorpio, Supermoon.

The Moon is on the opposite side of the Earth as the Sun, and its face will be fully illuminated. This phase occurs at 10:45 UTC. The May full moon is known as the Full Flower Moon because this was the time of year when spring flowers are in abundance. This full moon is also known as the Full Corn Planting Moon and the Milk Moon. This is also the last of four supermoons for 2020. The Moon will be at its closest approach to the Earth and looks slightly larger and brighter.

May 14 – Last Quarter Moon in Aquarius.

This Moon phase occurs at 14.03 UTC.

May 22 - New Moon in Taurus.

The Moon will be located on the same side of the Earth as the Sun and won't be seen in the night sky. This phase occurs at 17:39 UTC. The new moon phase is a brilliant time to observe galaxies and stars because there is no moonlight visible.

May 30 – First Quarter Moon in Virgo.

This Moon phase occurs at 3.30 UTC.

MAY HOROSCOPE

MAY WEEK ONE

This is an energizing time, the May 7th Supermoon leaves you feeling especially uplifted. It's time to spread your wings, an energizing phase offers you room to grow your social circle, it is a lovely chapter where you connect with like-minded people whose mindsets complement yours. It does bring interesting chemistry into play, making it an excellent time for brainstorming, developing new ideas, and expanding your creativity. This is an ideal time to plant original intentions which will unfold for you over the coming chapter. It does bring you in contact with a character you admire, and it also introduces you to new friends and fresh options which expand your social environment. Mingling with others does bring inspiration into your life, it is a refreshing time of creativity and self-expression ahead. You unpack a chapter which holds a great deal of potential within it. It does lift your spirits and lands you in an area which is ripe for progression. While it sees a higher demand on your time and energy, as developing long-term plans come into play, you can navigate the path ahead, even if it feels daunting, and by summoning your courage, you discover a lofty goal takes shape. Opportunities are likely to crop up, which enable you to progress essential goals. It leads to a productive chapter which provides you with impressive results. It is a crucial time where you move forward and make decisions that count. This sparks opportunities which are worth investigating, recognition, and achievement are also indicated.

MAY WEEK TWO

You soon ring in new opportunities, this takes you towards expansion, it enables you to see the broader world of possibilities which tempt you forward. A surge of optimism flows into your world, as a closer bond deepens with one who captures your imagination. It does see a shift which tugs at your heart, you feel encouraged by events on the horizon, this lets you become more confident about opening your heart to the potential possible. It is a time of incredible potential, an opportunity ahead invites you to learn a new area, this sees you launch your skills towards an endeavor which offers room to progress your talents. A phase of growth is imminent, it makes way for new inspiration, this motivates you to set your sights on a lofty goal. You can go after your dreams, and make it happen. There is news coming which is exciting, you welcome this information when it arrives, and it does have you discussing the future potential with another. This is a favorable influence which provides you with a path of inspiration. Taking time to go into the finer details will help make the most of this beautiful potential. The future is looking bright, it does indicate a pivotal time emerges, which enables you to make progress on creating substantial changes which progress your situation. This is a beautiful ticket to a fast-flowing environment which sees progression occurring quickly. It is a thrilling time, and as you start to see things pick up, you discover a trend which enables further growth is achievable. It is a happy phase which offers you new possibilities, it also blends well with your current situation, so it doesn't feel like an uncomfortable evolution, it brings new experiences and more prosperous emotional life. This creates the fresh start you have been seeking.

MAY WEEK THREE

It is a time where you can reflect on your goals, creating space to resolve outworn energy does open your life to new potential. Looking ahead, you soon attract the attention of someone who offers a refreshing change of pace. This person will have you reflecting on your goals, you may discover your priorities are shifting, and this expands your life and takes you to a time of new adventures. This relates to healing the past, a situation you were banking on may not have reached its full potential, and this has left you feeling a lingering sense of concern. It is time to create space and cleanse any residual negative emotions, this healing work is fundamental in releasing the past, and creating a shift which has you focused forward and ready to break new ground. You are entering a time which speeds up potential, it does bring changes and opportunities into your life, this opens the door to expanding your horizons. It is a time of fresh starts, and this can also bring up a sensitive stream of emotional awareness as you also deal with closing the door on a chapter that holds so many memories. Take time to reflect and ground your spirit. This is a time which can feel sentimental and emotional, you indicate over the past, and there are so many memories to pause and relive in your mind. He does say possible changes are arriving soon, this is a time where you can create a new path for yourself. It may also see added responsibility on your shoulders. This is an excellent time to focus on restoring balance. If you have felt a little off-kilter, spending time nurturing areas which hold meaning, will help ground and regain stability. There is an event coming soon, which offers you a chance to celebrate with other social types. It does help rejuvenate your spirit and ensures you can restore harmony.

MAY WEEK FOUR

You reach a crossroads soon, it does provide you with a great fresh start. You will likely feel a sense of purpose as you head in a direction which allows the right situation to surface. It has you discovering a delicate area to explore, and it helps dispel the pressure you have dealt with recently during an unsettling time of finding your balance again. Making the correct decision provides ample benefits soon after. Some changes are coming soon, which are going to be massive for your career path. Making the right decision sets the ball rolling on an expansive chapter. An offer arrives, and this news should be exciting and welcomed. It has you negotiating a path which rewards your talents and provides you with ample room to grow your situation. It does see you facing new duties and responsibilities. It is a pivotal time where you're able to create significant change. This comes about as a result of your analytical thinking, strategic planning, and ability to make the decisions which count. You discover that it is a busy time with various developments happening around you, which require your attention. Anticipating a couple of steps ahead will help you maintain balance as you move forward through this phase of expansion. Making a firm decision ahead, you begin to pick up speed on achieving your life goals. Improvement in your circumstances is a trend which gains more traction once you open your mind to the full potential possible. It is an energizing time, which is exciting and adventurous. Developments ahead support a chapter of growth as you embark on earning a new area, this has the potential to bring robust dividends to your world.

JUNE ASTROLOGY

June 4 - Mercury at Greatest Eastern Elongation.

The planet Mercury reaches greatest eastern elongation of 23.6 degrees from the Sun.

June 5 - Full Moon in Sagittarius.

The Full Moon is on the opposite side of the Earth as the Sun, and its face will be completely illuminated. This moon phase occurs at 19:12 UTC. This full moon is known as Full Strawberry Moon because it is the peak of the strawberry harvesting season. The June Full Moon has also been identified as the Full Rose Moon and the Full Honey Moon.

June 5 – Penumbral Lunar Eclipse.

This Moon eclipse occurs when the Moon passes through the Earth's partial shadow or penumbra. During this type of eclipse, the Moon will darken slightly but not completely disappear. This lunar eclipse will be visible throughout most of Europe, Africa, Asia, and Australia.

June 10 - Jupiter at Opposition.

The planet Jupiter will be at its nearest approach to Earth, and its planet face will be illuminated entirely by the Sun.

June 13 – Last Quarter Moon in Pisces.

This Moon phase occurs at 6.24 UTC.

June 17 – Mercury Retrograde begins in Cancer.

During a retrograde period, it isn't the right time to move forward in any practical venture. Be prepared for misunderstandings and miscommunications to be prevalent.

June 21 - June Solstice.

The June solstice occurs at 21:44 UTC. The North Pole will be tilted toward the Sun, which, having reached its northernmost position in the sky will be over the Tropic of Cancer at 23.44 degrees north latitude. This heralds the first day of summer (summer solstice) in the Northern Hemisphere, and is considered one of the most critical times of the year for many traditional cultures. It is the first day of winter (winter solstice) for the Southern Hemisphere.

June 21 - New Moon in Cancer.

The Moon is on the same side of the Earth as the Sun and will not be visible in the night sky. This moon phase occurs at 6:41 UTC. This is an excellent time to observe galaxies and stars because there is little moonlight to obstruct your view.

June 21 – Annual Solar Eclipse.

An annular solar eclipse occurs when the Moon is too far away from the Earth to completely cover the Sun. This results in a ring of light around the darkened Moon. The Sun's corona is not visible during an annular eclipse. The path of this solar eclipse begins in central Africa and travel through Saudi Arabia, northern India, and southern China before ending in the Pacific Ocean. A partial solar eclipse occurs throughout most of eastern Africa, the Middle East, and South Asia.

June 28 – First Quarter Moon in Libra.

This Moon phase occurs at 8.16 UTC.

JUNE HOROSCOPE

JUNE WEEK ONE

Taking time to build the path ahead carefully and with diligence and perseverance, offers you a chance to really make your mark on improving your situation. You begin to see clearly what is possible, and this becomes a dramatic tool for you to create the changes you are seeking. It does lead to a chapter of change and growth, it also indicates some sweet opportunities arrive to support your vision. Setting the bar high will provide you with the right environment to grow your dreams. There is someone ahead who lights up your personal life, it puts a strong emphasis on your love life and building a romance with someone who is a close friend. This person brings companionship into your life, they help you substantially grow your goals, it does suggest this situation arrives out of the blue, a beautiful surprise to light up your life. You negotiate a position which takes center stage in your life soon. It does more extensive in your options, you use communication to stunning effect to put your case forward. It is a thoughtful time where you are clear and concise about what you hope to achieve. This brings you an offer which enables you to make progress and forge ahead towards developing an area which shows promise. It does inspire you to expand your life.

JUNE WEEK TWO

The planet Jupiter reaches its closest approach to the earth this week. It will be at its brightest, and this illuminates a new direction. Jupiters influence is one of luck, expansion, and good fortune. Some upgrades are coming into your life soon. The path ahead it is paved with golden opportunities, having the right mindset, creating space to open your heart to a new situation, sets the right environment for a case to blossom soon after. There is healing coming into your life, it is a time of seeing the potential below the surface. Keeping your eye on your romantic goals does help you break new ground, and this draws new potential into your world. It brings a vital shift where you can ascertain the right moves to make to obtain progress. This is a great time, it advances your personal goals, leading to a time of healing, balancing your energy, and resolving outworn feelings, you do the emotional work necessary to shift your focus forward. Essential changes are coming, which benefit from contemplative insight and reflection. The more you understand your situation, the better you can stoke your vision, and put an action plan into place which sees potential soon follow.

JUNE WEEK THREE

The June 21st Solstice is an ideal time to pause and reflect on your goals. It is a new chapter which beckons and calls your name. There are areas to investigate which inspire your imagination, it does see you setting off on new adventures, you are likely to land in an exciting field, and this provides you with ample room to grow your situation. It is linked to good fortune, as well as the progression of a journey which occurs over time. This is a time where you can grow your goals. It does bring outcomes which enable you to successfully navigate a path which balances your current circumstances while building a bridge to where you want to be. It does debut a new venture, which offers a chance to flex your talents as you discover where they could take you. You're also likely to bump into an old friend soon. It is a time which beams positive energy into your life, it does lift your spirits and have you thinking about future possibilities with an optimistic mindset. This beautifully aligns you towards a sunny aspect, you deepen a situation, which offers a room to progress your personal goals. There may be additional jitters, as it takes you out of your comfort zone, as you discover a bond with one who is self-expressive and compassionate. It culminates in a chapter of increasing harmony. This opens a gateway towards growth. This person is charming, they are compelling and noble of heart. The sun is lighting a path forward, this chapter reveals hidden information which enables potential to rise to the surface. Hearing from this person provides you with clarity, it completes the cycle, which has been in motion for some time.

JUNE WEEK FOUR

Mercury Retrograde sees that this is a time where you can benefit from going within. There is an area you may have struggled with. Recently, wires have been crossed, miscommunication rife, it's all led to difficulties; however, this week does show that outworn energy can be resolved, releasing old patterns, creates space for a fresh flow of abundance to flow into your world. It does see potential heightened in your personal life, this leads to a big transition, there are some beautiful changes ahead, which boost your love life. There are some changes ahead for you, a substantial chapter begins with a sense of transformation. You connect with the one who heals the past, this person seeks to become closer, this shines a light on an area where you can begin to see potential flowing into your love life. It is a grounded time. New potential flows into your life, you discover things start to come together with someone who comes into your world, this person is endearing, they have a spirit which is generous and enriching, constructive dialogues take place which enables you to build a bond which is charming and soothing. You discover being with this person leaves you feeling peaceful and contented with life. It is an important gateway, crossing over, takes you towards a closer bond. You turn a corner in your life soon, and this lights a path of advancing abundance. It lets you head to a chapter which offers many blessings, it does feature new people emerging in your life, this expansion opens an option which draws joy into your world. You do discover a connection with the one who helps renew your spirit, it does see lively discussions with this person, tempting you forward.

JULY ASTROLOGY

July 5 - Full Moon in Capricorn.

The July Full Moon is located on the opposite side of the Earth as the Sun and will be fully illuminated. This phase occurs at 4:44 UTC. This full moon is known as Full Buck Moon because the male buck deer start to grow new antlers. This full moon is also known as the Full Thunder Moon and the Full Hay Moon.

July 5 – Penumbral Lunar Eclipse.

This Moon eclipse occurs when the Moon passes through the Earth's partial shadow or penumbra. During this type of eclipse, the Moon will darken slightly but not completely disappear. This lunar eclipse will be visible throughout most of Europe, Africa, Asia, and Australia.

July 12 – Last Quarter Moon in Aries.

This Moon phase occurs at 23.29 UTC.

July 12 - Mercury Retrograde ends in Cancer.

You can now move forward with any delayed plans that you have been putting off due to the Mercury Retrograde phase. Relationships should soon improve as communication improves.

July 14 - Jupiter at Opposition.

The Giant planet Jupiter will be at its nearest approach to Earth and will be at it's brightest.

July 20 - New Moon in Cancer.

The July New Moon is located on the same side of the Earth as the Sun and won't be visible in the night sky. This moon phase occurs at 17:33 UTC. This is an excellent time to observe galaxies and stars because there is no moonlight visible.

July 20 - Saturn at Opposition.

The beautiful ringed planet Saturn will be at its nearest approach to Earth and will be illuminated by the Sun.

July 22 - Mercury at Greatest Western Elongation.

The planet Mercury reaches greatest western elongation of 20.1 degrees from the Sun.

July 27 – First Quarter Moon in Scorpio.

This Moon phase occurs at 12.32 UTC.

July 28, 29 - Delta Aquarids Meteor Shower.

The Delta Aquarids meteor shower peaks on the night of July 28 and morning of July 29. The first quarter moon may block many of the fainter meteors this year. You should still be able to view the brighter ones. Best viewing will be at a dark vista after midnight. Meteors radiate from the constellation Aquarius but can appear anywhere in the sky.

JULY HOROSCOPE

JULY WEEK ONE

The full moon this week connects you to your intuition and higher wisdom. You may be processing recent events, this can lead to sensitivities arising, and you may discover, you need to reshuffle your commitments and take time to catch your breath. There is a lot to integrate, this is an opportunity to reflect, and gain introspection into the path ahead. Slowing down enables you to ground and center your spirit, taking inventory is highly effective, and provides emotional sustenance. There is support around you, you are headed towards a chapter laced with expansion, honesty, and growth. It is a theme which nourishes your soul and enables your spirit to blossom in fertile ground. Getting back to basics, you honor the most fiercely independent aspect of your vision. Liberating yourself from the constraints of everyday life harnesses the power of adventure to put the spark in your life. You are being supported to reach for an area which draws abundance into your world. This helps release the sense of anxiety, which may be holding you back. You may have been feeling weighed down by all the demands on your energy, this is set to change, and you release the tension that has been swirling around you, this sends it packing, a fresh perspective and mindset provide you with beautiful inspiration. A goal you are working towards becomes a much bigger focus, seeing things dart forward, which adds an extra dose of motivation.

JULY WEEK TWO

Mercury Retrograde ends on the 12th of July, and this sees you successfully emerge from a cocoon where you have sheltered your creativity recently. Life becomes a whirlwind of potential, it sweeps through your life and heightens the emotional abundance possible. Turning to a friend for inspiration, you discover a closer bond is possible. It flips the potential, life takes on a new hue, under this gossamer lens, you find out a personal situation can blossom. It does launch you towards a chapter of magic and has you finding the perfect algorithm to improve your life. This is a rare and auspicious time where you find out clarification on an area which had been of concern, this rectifies a situation once thought to be problematic. It does ring in a time of news and developments which relates to illuminating a path ahead. It gives you a vision of future possibilities, and this inspires positive change, you discover an area beckons and using your gifts to help others leads to an expansion in your social life. There is some epic activity coming into your personal life. It does lead to a change-making a chapter, you get down to business about what your goals are, and begin to gain insight into how to achieve the highest potential. Making lofty resolutions provides you with the air of manifestation, it helps nurture your spirit in a way that provides you with a wonderful, "can do" attitude. It brings a long-overdue resolution to improve your love life. This is a lovely time to focus on nurturing yourself. Giving a gift of sustenance to your spirit does help you reach new levels of awareness. It creates an environment which draws abundance into your world. Something new unfolds in your life soon to give your metabolism a lovely lift, this boost, unites your mind and heart most gloriously.

JULY WEEK THREE

News arrives from someone you haven't heard from for quite some time. This person is kindhearted, deeply honorable, they possess a powerful intellect which makes them highly articulate and insightful. They are skilled at using their words carefully, and at choosing the right time to reconnect with you. They have lovely energy to their personality, which sees them delight in nurturing a closer bond, this is irrepressible and delightful. You discover there is more to a situation then meets the eye, this brings news which provides you with clarity about the past. This is a time which ignites grand possibilities and sets the stage for you to enter an incredible chapter of expansion. There are opportunities to move out of your everyday routine and try new things. It does give you plenty to contemplate, and having a variety of options is highly motivational, it shifts your focus forward and enables you to integrate the changes ahead in a beneficial fashion. You are ready to enter an expansive chapter, which fuels your life with self-expression and creativity. It brings a rush of potential into your life, and heralds, a sudden event or news arriving to inspire a surge of activity. It is a time where information comes out of the blue, and you feel you can achieve stellar outcomes by following your inspiration. It does highlight an aspect of adventure and excitement.

JULY WEEK FOUR

There are a lot of shifts ahead, some of them take in long term goals, and it gives you an entirely different perspective of your situation. It does see you switching to a new area, and this happens against a backdrop of feeling unsettled and working on getting a foothold on a trajectory which provides you with the stability you are seeking. Movement and progression are the order of the day, which connects you to a larger cycle of abundance. You are ready to embrace a new chapter which sees you get in touch with a goal that is close to your heart. Focusing on an important aspect does set the right intention, it provides terrific energy to motivate and encourage you to progress your dreams. There is a creative solution ahead, which helps you launch your situation forward. It brings more happiness into your world. It is a time where you surround yourself with people who resonate the best kind of energy. It is an energizing chapter which sees your potential amplified. A new situation emerges, which makes room for creative collaboration, it does lead to a curious phase where you connect with a kindred person who shares thoughtful conversations with you. This is someone who is in the lead to become a strong ally.

AUGUST ASTROLOGY

August 3 - Full Moon in Aquarius.

The August Full Moon is located on the opposite side of the Earth as the Sun and will be fully illuminated. This phase occurs at 15:59 UTC. The August full moon is known as the Full Sturgeon Moon because sturgeon fish of the Great Lakes and other major lakes were quickly caught during this time. This full moon has also been known as the Green Corn Moon and the Grain Moon.

August 11 – Last Quarter Moon in Taurus.

This Moon phase occurs at 16.45 UTC.

August 12, 13 - Perseids Meteor Shower.

The Perseids meteor shower runs each year from July 17 to August 24. It peaks this year on the night of August 12 and the morning of August 13. The Perseids meteor shower is one of the best to view as the meteors are so bright and numerous. The best viewing is from a dark vista after midnight.

August 13 - Venus at Greatest Western Elongation.

The planet Venus reaches greatest western elongation of 45.8 degrees from the Sun.

August 19 - New Moon in Leo.

The Moon will be on the same side of the Earth as the Sun and will not be visible in the night sky. This moon phase occurs at 2:41 UTC. This is an excellent time to observe galaxies and stars because there is no moonlight to obstruct the view.

August 25 – First Quarter Moon in Scorpio.

This Moon phase occurs at 17.58 UTC.

AUGUST HOROSCOPE

AUGUST WEEK ONE

August is the time to shine, you discover it is a richly creative phase, it warms your sense of self-expression and highlights artistic abilities which seek to emerge. Immersing yourself fully in an area which catches your interest is your most direct path to drawing abundance into your life. It helps you follow your heart and release stress. Look for signs that you need to slow down and rejuvenate your spirit. If you have been going forward at a hectic pace, this is a time to focus on self-care, and getting back to the basics, which allow you that wonderful sense of healing. Creating space to clean the slate does indeed lead to improvement further down the track. Addressing any issues now will allow you to move forward gracefully. You can let go of old hurts soon, this cathartic release arrives to take you to a time of healing enclosure. Letting go of outworn energy radically turns the tide is in your favor. It takes you towards a revolutionary chapter, where you make swift progress on a situation which had felt stagnant. You literally go with the flow and embrace developing a position which offers room for growth. You have done a fantastic job of arranging the demands on your time, but if you have felt burdened by events which have added to your life, you can pick up the pace, and break down areas into smaller commitments. Taking care of yourself first and foremost is vital in being able to keep up with other regions. You embrace some downtime soon where you can renew your energy.

AUGUST WEEK TWO

You escape in a field of wonder lust soon. Exploring creative possibilities opens an expanse of potential, which captures your inspiration. It syncs you up with an ambitious area that offers room for progress. It is an idyllic time where you pursue your dreams and develop unique areas which are perfect for your life. It does see you hitting your sweet spot, and kicks off a phase of growth. This is a fabulous time to forge ahead towards developing a new area. You enter uncharted territory which expands the potential ready to emerge in your life. It does help you create space to travel through a path which is enterprising, creative, and visionary. As you pull back the curtain on this energizing phase, you can embrace an exciting time which draws abundance. You enter a dynamic phase which removes deep-seated blocks. It helps you push back the boundaries which have curtailed your progress recently. Any speed bumps or obstacles soon fade away, you leave them in the dust of your inspiration. Your thirst for adventure sees you investing your energy in an exciting area that offers you room to grow your goals. This rejuvenates your spirit and is a beautiful signpost to follow. An intriguing option crops up for you soon. It kicks off a chapter which offers you new potential, it does see one of your goals being expanded, and the way things come together feels serendipitous. This synchronicity foretells of an auspicious time which feels connected with a more extensive array of abundance. It does help you capitalize on this exciting chapter of good fortune.

AUGUST WEEK THREE

You are ready to kick off a heart-opening phase, which centers around improving your home situation, as well as building deeply emotional foundations. It does see changes ahead, which open a door towards improvement in your life. As you dive the depths of the possibilities which surround you, it brings news of an essential change to your situation, which draws abundance into your world. You are ready to reinstate some boundaries, gently and firmly steer a personal situation in a direction which is in alignment with your heart. It does bring much-needed relief to your home life, and you begin to feel the momentum returning to your inspiration. This leads to a lighter chapter that focuses on improving some outstanding bonds in your life. Enticing news arrives to tempt you towards expansion. It does shift your focus forward, it's a fascinating, trailblazing chapter where you attract some dynamic people into your life. It does lead to the right collaborations, lively conversations, grab your attention, and you focus on one who is magnetizing and passionate. This person's idealistic nature provides you with an inspiring path, it could see a significant turning point in your life. Your social life is ripe for expansion, it does show you expressing yourself openly with one who catches your interest. The dialogues shared are pure and heartfelt, it leads to a fertile time where you can grow your dreams. It is a chapter which brings surprises, it rules the expansion of romance in your personal life. You discover you have the courage to push back the barriers and go after a bond with one who inspires your mind and your heart.

AUGUST WEEK FOUR

There may be someone in your life who is a little erratic and unpredictable, setting boundaries with this person will help restore your balance. You are doing the right thing by focusing on improving your situation, soon, you head to a chapter which holds promise. A secret is revealed, this gives you the clarity needed to heal the past, it brings you towards a shift forward. You are ready to embrace an exciting adventure of freedom and liberation. Currently, you are transitioning towards a glorious new chapter. As you stand at the crossroads, you feel uncertain about shifting your focus forward, this is natural, but you can trust your intuition to tap into the higher path, and guide you correctly. Your emotional awareness knows that a fresh start will do wonders for your soul. You are set to benefit from new opportunities which flow into your world to light the way forward. As you hit your stride, you discover you can expand your options and develop your dreams with a lovely rhythm that maintains balance while strengthening your goals. The foundations provide you with ample opportunities to weave blessings into your life, it does see some big doors open for you soon. You head towards a chapter which builds your goals. Enticing options cross your path, as you gather the threads of potential, you weave a basket of your dreams. It does take you towards a life chapter which heralds new possibilities supporting your higher growth. Following your heart leads to soul-expanding experiences, you realize that being an open vessel does create space for enjoyable new endeavors to call your name.

SEPTEMBER ASTROLOGY

September 2 - Full Moon in Pisces.

The September full Moon is on the opposite side of the Earth as the Sun, and its face will be fully illuminated. This phase occurs at 5:22 UTC. This full moon is known as the Full Corn Moon because the corn is harvested around this time.

September 10 – Last Quarter Moon in Gemini.

This Moon phase occurs at 9.26 UTC.

September 11 - Neptune at Opposition.

The giant blue planet will be at its closest approach to Earth, and its face will be illuminated by the Sun.

September 17 - New Moon in Virgo.

The Moon is on the same side of the Earth as the Sun and will not be visible in the night sky. This phase occurs at 11:00 UTC. This is an excellent time to observe galaxies and stars because there is no moonlight visible.

September 22 - September Equinox.

The 2020 September equinox occurs at 13:31 UTC. The Sun shines directly on the equator, creating equal amounts of day and night throughout the world. This is also the first day of fall (autumnal equinox) in the northern hemisphere and is considered a significant zodiac event for many traditional cultures.

September 24 – First Quarter Moon in Capricorn.

This Moon phase occurs at 1.55 UTC.

SEPTEMBER HOROSCOPE

SEPTEMBER WEEK ONE

Striking out in a new area culminates in a role which inspires your mind. It's a huge turning point, it harnesses your innovation and creativity to good effect. You soon begin to see tangible results, and you get a better idea of your true talents. It does suggest an offer crosses your path and points you in the right direction at the right time. This synchronicity is guiding your way towards achieving a substantial goal. Fresh winds blow into your life soon. It does create a stir of excitement, you discover there is someone around you who is a powerful ally, this person takes proactive steps to build a closer bond. It does have you shifting your thoughts forward and considering the potential possible. As you move out of your comfort zone, you embrace a comprehensive vision of opportunity. Positive changes stir a flow of creativity which offer new dreams. Bonuses are arriving for you soon, excitement and new possibilities make for a beautiful chapter filled with energy and adventure. It does have you striving to achieve specific goals which have been on the back burner for some time. As you enter a phase of growth, expansion, and potential, a surge of inspiration flows into your life to support building your dreams. You reveal some enticing new options soon, an offer crosses your path which provides you with a track that shines brightly. It underscores a theme of abundance, which is currently building in your life. The intensity of the past makes way for a light-hearted chapter. It does bring a chance to focus on your goals and dreams. Beginning a new venture draws a phase of inspiration, you are motivated to succeed.

SEPTEMBER WEEK TWO

The planet Neptune is at its closest approach to Earth this week, it will be at its brightest. Neptune rules your house of dreams and healing. News is imminent, which features a blessing in disguise. It can feel like a paradox, a chapter ends, but this also creates a beginning which enables you to shift your focus forward. Releasing something outworn makes way for new experiences to come rushing in. You quickly get started on a blank slate which offers you the potential to create an incredible chapter of abundance. Discovering new options is a remedy for your restless spirit. Changes ahead strike an excellent balance between your current situation and a bridge to expansion. You progress your life and still maintain those stable foundations which are so important in your world. It is an ideal time to explore new paths, your life takes on a hue of abundance under a creative landscape. It does see you traveling forward in alignment with your higher goals. An opportunity to bring your gifts to life brings joy. You take a lot on board and aligning your energy towards the areas which offer you the highest potential will help prevent you from becoming frayed and burning out before you reach completion of your goals. Syncing up with kindred spirits will take you to a zone of rejuvenation, this is extremely helpful for your situation, building strong social ties is therapeutic. This is an ideal type to revisit the past, reunite with reflection, and renew your spirit. Being done with outworn energy helps draw that line in the sand, it inspires you to create space to bring something new into your world. This is an essential factor in attracting new opportunities, in fact, an offer crops up soon to sweep through your life, radically shifting the tides in your favor.

SEPTEMBER WEEK THREE

News arrives, which resets the potential surrounding you. It takes a moment to recalibrate and get with this new evolution of growth. You may feel drawn to initiating a significant change, and feel uncertain about the next steps to take. This path illuminates a way forward, keeping your long term goals in mind, does plot the strategic course to a destination which draws abundance. Creativity and imagination blaze brightly in this fascinating landscape. This sets the tone for an energizing chapter, your romantic situation may have been slowed down recently, and if you have worried about it stalling, the changes ahead are actually an opportunity to shift things forward, you get clear on what can be achieved with your love life. You take on a trajectory, which is more focused, goal orientated, and driven. It does keep things light-hearted at the same time and offers opportunities to explore creative solutions. It is a time where you can navigate any rough patches, and work on drawing renewal into your life. If you have felt on the verge of burnout, life becomes slower, more focused on achieving light-hearted ambiance. It does bring you back to basics, and create space to heal any frayed edges which have limited your growth recently. This healing cycle puts you in touch with your larger goals. It is a productive time which lights up an aspect of self-expression. It takes you towards developing a closer connection with someone meaningful. This leads to an adventurous chapter, and it does hit the sweet spot, providing you with plenty of inspiration. There is a shift forward that gives you a source of inspiration. It marks a bold new beginning and sets you on a path of exploration. A willingness to initiate change does see you investing your energy in a good situation. It brings confidence, and give you a sneak peek of future possibilities.

SEPTEMBER WEEK FOUR

The Equinox this week arrives to allow you the ability to harness the power of manifestation. It illuminates a fantastic path where you can bring your goals together with a flourish. It does take you to a time of being around groups and teams, a collaborative approach does seem the order of the day in this new role. It gears you up to launch towards being more involved in your working life. You may even take on an inspiring leadership role, which sees you sharing your wisdom with others. You establish a position of authority and respect, restrictions which have been an issue recently are lifted. This sees a fast-moving progression occurring, it may prompt you to take a look at your business plans, and see where you can pull in areas, and jumpstart other areas which heightened productivity. You begin to see those rock-solid foundations are emerging, and this gives you a sense that things are progressing nicely. You have many gifts to share with the world, and your creative offerings are going to take you places. You have grown a lot over the last few years, emotionally, spiritually, and creatively. A time of transformation does take you towards building your dreams, and it helps you heal from the knocks you have made in the past. Your third eye is getting back to a higher vision, and this will guide you. Things are on the move for you. This leads to a time where you gently get back in your groove, as you begin to send those feelers out, which have you exploring new areas to tap into. It does sync you up with an ambitious phase, this brings you to a time where you can plot a course towards achieving a long-term goal. Learning a new area may also cross your path soon. This is a time which kicks off a chapter of rejuvenation, it brings new foundations, and it does see you improving your living situation.

OCTOBER ASTROLOGY

October 1 - Full Moon in Aries.

The October full Moon is on the opposite side of the Earth as the Sun, and its face will be fully illuminated. This phase occurs at 21:05 UTC. This full moon is known as the Hunters Moon because at this time of year the leaves are falling, and the game is ready. This full moon is also known as the Travel Moon and the Blood Moon. This moon is also known as the Harvest Moon. The Harvest Moon is the full moon that occurs closest to the September equinox each year.

October 1 - Mercury at Greatest Eastern Elongation.

The planet Mercury reaches greatest eastern elongation of 25.8 degrees from the Sun.

October 7 - Draconids Meteor Shower.

The Draconids meteor shower runs annually from October 6-10 and peaks this year on the night of the 7th.

October 10 – Last Quarter Moon in Cancer.

This Moon phase occurs at 0.39 UTC.

October 13 – Mercury Retrograde begins in Scorpio.

During a retrograde period, it isn't the right time to move forward in any practical venture. Be prepared for misunderstandings and miscommunications to be more prevalent.

October 16 - New Moon in Libra.

The Moon will be on the same side of the Earth as the Sun and will not be seen in the night sky. This moon phase occurs at 19:31 UTC. This is an excellent time of the month to view galaxies and stars because there is no moonlight visible.

October 21, 22 - Orionids Meteor Shower.

The Orionids meteor shower runs yearly from October 2 to November 7. Orionids meteor shower peaks this year on the night of October 21 and the morning of October 22.

October 23 – First Quarter Moon in Capricorn.

This Moon phase occurs at 13.23 UTC.

October 31 - Full Moon, Blue Moon in Taurus.

The October full Blue Moon is on the opposite side of the Earth as the Sun, and its face will be fully illuminated. This phase occurs at 14:49 UTC. This is the second full moon in the same month, it is referred to as a blue moon.

October 31 - Uranus at Opposition.

The planet Uranus will be at its nearest approach to Earth, and its face will be illuminated by the Sun.

OCTOBER HOROSCOPE

OCTOBER WEEK ONE

A situation that has been building for some time starts to take on a life of its own. You discover you can move forward to a more grounded phase with someone special. Engaging proactively in sharing thoughts and ideas does light up the potential for growth, and you discover this person is willing to adapt and compromise, to keep the situation developing and evolving. Overall, the landscape ahead is improving. News arrives, out of the blue, it sees a shift in potential which illuminates an enticing path. You develop an area which captures your imagination, it connects you with your more significant dreams and goals. You lift the lid on the situation which simmers with exciting potential. As you unfurl the gifts ahead, you get a useful scope on where you are headed, and how best to achieve an active phase of growth. You enter an expansive phase which sees you emerge from the cocoon, you direct your skills towards an area which offers room for growth. It does see you taking on a role which picks up speed, you grow your talents, and this does invite new offers to your table to contemplate. It also brings changes to your personal life, all indications point to the start of a significant new chapter, this shows an outlook which is brighter, more expressive. This is a glorious time to expand your life and bring something new to experience. It is a highly social aspect, a new venture leads to long talks with other kindred spirits. Sharing your ideas and point of view creates a beautiful brew of potential. You glean a path which highlights growth and progression.

OCTOBER WEEK TWO

You are someone who thrives in a busy environment, you have so many interests and curiosities, it inspires your mind to stay active. Expanding your horizons, you discover there is a rich landscape to explore, follow your imagination, and plunge into the creative depths which call your name. It does awaken the sense of adventure and leads to a time of discovery. It is a time of heightened activity in your social life, your situation soars to new heights, following your intuition, you connect with one person who gels well with your life. It may even feel fated or karmic, lively discussions with this person also illuminates new dimensions of your own personality. This is someone who helps you discover a broad range of areas, this is a person who is focused on building a strong bond. Things are on the move, it does see a transit where you can release doubts, de-clutter anxious thoughts, and begin to focus on developing a path which is in alignment with your long-term goals. This takes you towards a chapter which is highly organized, and it is a boon for your stability. There are a lot of options coming up, which draw good fortune into your world. It gives you ample inspiration to explore. An offer crops up, which feels like a good fit. It sparks a productive chapter, which gets you thinking outside of the box. Expanding your horizons does broaden the options available. It takes you to a time of building stable foundations and gently moving forward.

OCTOBER WEEK THREE

There may be tension in your life, demands on your time pull you between work, home, and other commitments. However, things should ease up soon, this beautifully aligns you towards a more light-hearted phase, where you can take some much-needed downtime to rejuvenate your spirit. It is also a highly artistic time, which gives way to new methods of self-expression. You may find yourself picking up the pieces after a difficult chapter. It is a cathartic time where you can focus on healing as you prepare to begin a new chapter. Seven is a magic number, it helps you pick up speed, and does draw fresh opportunities into your life. Under the influence of this, you enter a time of personal growth and evolution. There are some changes ahead where you release areas which have held back your progress. It does see the sun shining brightly in your social aspect. This indicates it's an excellent time to catch up with friends, and it does see invitations arriving to support spending time with your closest ties. It is a shift forward, where you can focus on a significant situation, this brings a buzz of excitement into your life, as news arrives, which inspires your mind. A smart and insightful person helps open the door for you to progress a larger goal that you have been working towards. This is someone you haven't heard from for quite some time. It does see new potential brewing, this person brings their thoughts out in the open, and it gives you a sneak preview of where this situation could head. A lot of old emotional energy comes pouring out, this is someone who really begins to dig deep and tell you how they have been feeling. It does ignite a fresh chapter of possibilities.

OCTOBER WEEK FOUR

The rare Full Blue Moon this week says it is a time of abundance and magic. You have so many different interests and curiosities that it is difficult to know which path to develop. This can have you feeling out of your depth and feeling overwhelmed by the choices available. There is a rich landscape to explore, your imagination and intuition will help guide you towards choosing the right area to explore. You discover your sense of adventure awakens to a rich landscape of potential soon. It is a time where you tie up some loose ends, reflecting, and integrating the chapter which has recently occurred. As you pause and reflect on the past, you activate a sense of renewal. It does create space to release outmoded areas and resolve any feelings which are holding you back. This creates a beautiful environment for drawing something new into your life. Opportunities soon come knocking to tempt you forward. You may be processing difficult emotions, shining the light on what is happening in your world, helps bring up areas which can be worked on and resolved. If you have learned some tough lessons this year, those hard knocks are going to smooth out and make way for a more settled and balanced chapter. Keep moving, opportunities are around the corner. Any self-improvement started this month will draw a booster of motivation into your life. It has you feeling rejuvenated, and this renewal hits a sweet spot. It opens at gateway towards a chapter which is vibrant, eclectic, and social. Maintaining forward motion, you spend time with other kindred spirits you harmonize your life. This is a time where you can relax and enjoy.

NOVEMBER ASTROLOGY

November 3 - Mercury Retrograde ends in Libra.

You can now move forward with any delayed plans that you have been putting off due to the Mercury Retrograde phase. Relationships should soon improve as miscommunications resolve.

November 4, 5 - Taurids Meteor Shower.

The Taurids meteor shower runs yearly from September 7 to December 10. It peaks this year on the night of November 4.

November 8 – Last Quarter Moon in Leo.

This Moon phase occurs at 13.46 UTC.

November 15 - New Moon in Scorpio.

The Moon is on the same side of the Earth as the Sun and will not be visible in the night sky. This phase occurs at 5:07 UTC. This is an excellent time to view galaxies and star clusters because there is no moonlight visible.

November 17, 18 - Leonids Meteor Shower.

The Leonids meteor shower runs yearly from November 6-30. The Leonids meteor shower peaks this year on the night of the 17th and morning of the 18th.

November 22 – First Quarter Moon in Pisces.

This Moon phase occurs at 4.45 UTC.

November 30 - Full Moon in Gemini.

The November full Moon is on the opposite side of the Earth as the Sun, and its face will be fully illuminated. This phase occurs at 9:30 UTC. This full moon is known as Full Beaver Moon as this was the time of year to set beaver traps before the swamps and rivers froze. It is also known as the Frosty Moon and the Hunter's Moon.

November 30 - Penumbral Lunar Eclipse

A penumbral lunar eclipse occurs when the Moon passes through the Earth's partial shadow or penumbra. During this type of eclipse, the Moon will darken but not completely eclipse. This Penumbral lunar eclipse will be visible throughout most of North America, the Pacific Ocean, and northeastern Asia.

NOVEMBER HOROSCOPE

NOVEMBER WEEK ONE

The Taurids meteor shower which peaks on November 4th shines brightly with abundance. It shows a time where you can progress a goal which is close to your heart. It enables you to feel as though you are on track, and able to grow an area which holds meaning to you. Your creativity soars to new heights, along with your intuition, this enables you to dismantle any blocks which have prevented progress, it leads to new discoveries which inspire growth. It does show a new chapter is coming, which harnesses a time of clarity, it marks the start of a branch which is insightful, and has you busy planning for future growth. A bond becomes essential to focus, developing a situation that holds a meeting to you consumes a great deal of your energy in the chapter ahead. It leads to moments which are fresh and beautiful, a thoughtful gesture takes on new meaning. It is a time which inspires growth, you may feel drawn to learning a new area, it rules an aspect of revealing new knowledge, and bringing information to light, which will offer you a chance to grow your talents. You get involved in a community setting, it leads to social time and helps you discover new outlets for your creativity. You head to a vibrant time where you feel ready to explore new ideas, putting your dreams front and center, does give you a creative outlet which draws expansive and healing energy into your life. It leads to a happy chapter, which has you moving in alignment with your larger goals. This is a transformational time, it involves healing the past, and bringing your gifts to light. In fact, you could be reaching a much wider audience soon.

NOVEMBER WEEK TWO

As you chart a course towards spending time with others, you discover a mentor and helpful person who opens doors, this is someone you can lean on for guidance, this one does help you clarify your ideas, and bring valuable information to light. Taking stock of where you currently are, enables you to chart a course correctly towards an active phase of growth. Utilizing strategy and planning is key to taking proactive steps towards achieving your goals. It is a time where you can improve your life, it helps close the gap between your dreams and goals, and your current situation. Planning concrete steps to work towards, sees you spending time with someone who does wonders for your spirit. It is a lighthearted chapter which offers opportunities to collaborate with a kindred spirit. Fascinating dialogues create the right blend for creative inspiration. This person is a valuable ally, it does have you surrounding yourself with the right kind of energy to support your goals. It lands you squarely in an aspect, which combines romance and creativity. A connection which has been brewing offers exciting moments which touch your heart. It is a memorable month which shines a light on developing a closer bond with a vibrant personality who inspires you. It does create an exciting mix of potential, you feel the light shining on your life. It offers you a chance to share your ideas, and spend time creating plans for future growth. This is a month which activates new potential, and it unleashes fresh possibilities which can improve your personal life. As you sift through various options, you create a beautiful blend of ideas with one who offers sage advice.

NOVEMBER WEEK THREE

Things are going to be improving soon. It creates a shift forward, which amplifies your potential, you can leave issues and drama behind in the dust of your inspiration. This serves up a phase which offers you room to grow your dreams. It takes you towards an adventure where you can enjoy life with spirit and abandon. A glimpse of future possibilities arrives soon to snag your attention. A fantastic opportunity comes in the form of an offer. This gives you an overview of where your dreams are headed, you consider this option a lucky break. Listening to your emotional awareness, taps into a wellspring of inspiration. You're motivated to make things happen, and this is a time which grabs your attention and gets you looking at the bigger picture surrounding your aspirations. An upgrade is coming to your life soon, this gives you a clue about future possibilities. A theme of abundance is beginning to grow in fertile ground. You may discover energy from the past also resurfaces, this is a transitional phase, it brings up unresolved issues which seek your attention to help sweep aside outworn areas, you then create space for an empowering new chapter to spring to life. This is a time which brings back a sense of optimism, it gives you a powerful feeling that things are working in your favor. It is a bond which rejuvenates your soul and has you envisioning future possibilities. There is plenty of activity to shift this forward, it does take you towards building foundations which draw energy from your nurturing and caring aspect. News arrives soon to light the path ahead.

NOVEMBER WEEK FOUR

This week brims with new potential. You scope out an area which offers you room to harness a creative aspect. It gets you busy visualizing and manifesting, this taps into an area which inspires your mind. It does lead to more social time, invitations to mingle, put you in contact with other like-minded individuals. It is a month which illuminates harmony, and happy moments which balance and bless your life. This hits a sweet spot in your personal life. It offers you a chance to develop a situation which provides you with a sense of excitement and adventure. It does see forward motion in a few critical areas of your life. Amidst a hectic backdrop, you discover there is time to pause and reflect on the changes which are surrounding your life. There are many blessings to appreciate, and this month is a game-changer for you. There are definite indications that you will achieve a personal goal soon. Obtaining a new chapter enables you to feel grounded, it provides you with a superb choice to expand your life. This put you in a strong position to start planning for future growth. It's important to give yourself time to settle into this new landscape, it does reconnect you to the basics, and provides you with a clean slate to start fresh. You are likely to enter a phase of transformation, this leads to a stunning breakthrough, it combines dynamic chemistry with a blend of artistic expression. The changes ahead provide you with a powerful option, one that feels synchronistic, meant to be. This is a time which squarely places you in a phase of expansion where you can reboot your energy and rejuvenate your spirit.

DECEMBER ASTROLOGY

December 8 – Last Quarter Moon in Virgo.

This Moon phase occurs at 0.37 UTC.

December 13, 14, 15 - Geminids Meteor Shower.

The Geminids meteor shower runs each year from December 7-17. The Geminids meteor showers peaks this year on the night of the 13th, 14th, and 15th. The nearly new moon this year will provide dark skies for an excellent show. Best viewing will be from a dim vista after midnight. Meteors will radiate from the constellation Gemini but can appear anywhere in the sky.

December 14 - New Moon in Sagittarius.

The Moon is on the same side of the Earth as the Sun and will not be visible in the night sky. This moon phase occurs at 16:17 UTC. This is an excellent time to view galaxies and stars because there is no moonlight visible.

December 21 – First Quarter Moon in Pisces.

This Moon phase occurs at 23.41 UTC.

December 21 - December Solstice.

The 2020 December solstice occurs at 10:02 UTC. The South Pole of the earth tilts toward the Sun, which, having reached its most southern place in the sky, is directly over the Tropic of Capricorn at 23.44 degrees south latitude. This December solstice also marks the first day of winter (winter solstice) in the Northern Hemisphere.

December 21 – Great Conjunction of Jupiter and Saturn.

A conjunction of Jupiter and Saturn will take place on December 21. This is known as the great conjunction as it is a rare celestial event. The last great conjunction occurred in the year 2000. The two bright planets will appear only 7 arc minutes of each other in the night sky. They will be so close that they will seem to make a bright double planet. Look to the west just after sunset for this impressive and rare planetary pair.

December 21, 22 - Ursids Meteor Shower.

The Ursids meteor shower occurs each year from December 17 - 25. This meteor event peaks this year on the night of the 21st and morning of the 22nd.

December 30 - Full Moon in Cancer.

The Moon is on the opposite side of the Earth as the Sun, and its face will be fully illuminated. This moon phase occurs at 03:28 UTC. This full moon is known as the Full Cold Moon because this is the time of year when the cold winters air arrives and nights become long and dark. This full moon can also be known as the Long Nights Moon and the Moon Before Yule.

DECEMBER HOROSCOPE

DECEMBER WEEK ONE

December hits the right kind of positive note that you need in your life. It brings an exciting opportunity to expand your options. This connects you with like-minded people, a group approach helps you discover firsthand how you can grow your goals, and it leads to a more social chapter which has you spending time with people who are on the same wavelength. It does boost your potential and draws rejuvenation to your spirit. You have an excellent domestic side which nurtures matters of home and heart. There are many traditions in your past, which hold significant meaning. While you have many plans for future growth, taking on too much at once is draining for you. Take time to embrace the moment, there is a wellspring of abundance already surrounding your life. Invitations arrive to help spread your social wings soon. You ring in a successful outcome which draws plenty into your world. You discover opportunity comes calling, it reminds you to take time to progress personal goals, you enjoy the lightness of life, your social life gets a reboot. This enables you to spend time with the person who captures your fancy, it leads to a phase which pushes back boundaries, it shines a spotlight on increasing intimacy and the development of bonds. You discover fantastic communication is on the agenda with one who is diplomatic, inspiring, and magnetic. It does have you set your sights on developing a bond which offers room to progress your personal goals. This could bring an opportunity to merge with one who inspires your mind. It does see you focus shift to long-term goals.

DECEMBER WEEK TWO

This week reveals that there is support available within your more full social circle. You are doing the right thing by not settling for short-term goals. Opportunities support your vision, there is a seed which is set to blossom over the coming months, as this is yet to unfold, you can take your time and allow things to progress gently in the fullness of time. Long-term security is spotlighted as a theme which draws abundance into your world. It is a time which brings a considerable boon to your creativity, it helps you chart a course towards an endeavor which is a lofty, yet doable. As you reach a pinnacle of sorts, you gain a broader perspective of the abundance of which is seeking to emerge in your life. You do discover a bond with one whose talents compliments yours. It does provide you with a sense of thrilling possibilities and exciting adventures yet to come. There is an out of the blue opportunity which crosses your path and sees you getting more involved in a community setting. This offers you a wellspring of abundance, you connect well with others during this social chapter. It does see you moving out of your usual comfort zone and embracing a lighthearted phase which draws happy moments into your world. It is a blissful time which offers you new adventures to explore. There is an area where you invest your energy that provides ample room for progression. It is an endeavor which draws blessings into your world and also delivers incredible outcomes to a broader audience. Something started at this time will gently unfold over the coming months, taking those first initial steps, clears the space for a new progression of potential to inspire your mind.

DECEMBER WEEK THREE

You enter a grounded chapter soon, which brings the balance back into your life. Restoring and renewing your spirit brings you back in sync with other opportunities that surround your world. It does plant your goals in solid ground, it offers you a chance to expand your horizons, which culminates in an exciting offer crossing your path soon, things to come together with a flourish. Any indecisiveness, which is currently holding you back, will be dissolved and released. It takes you to a grounded second half of this year, you keep things simple and sweet, and build your goals in a manageable fashion. It does have you hitting new areas to develop, and this cranks up your creativity, it underscores a theme of abundance which is seeking to blossom in your world. Given a chance to grow, you truly shine. You slide into a new role soon. This offers you an excellent opportunity to embrace a chapter which sees you enjoying the rewards for all the hard work you have done before. It plants you on fertile ground, it enables you to build foundations which offer security. It is a reasonable time which initiates the building of a framework that will continue to fill out further down the line. You have such a great deal of control over the path ahead. Directing your focused thoughts and intentions correctly does intensify the energy of manifestation available to you. It sees a return to your old spirited self, it is an expressive time, which gives you the confidence to expand your boundaries and live life to the fullest. It is a shift forward, which offers you inspiration and success.

DECEMBER WEEK FOUR

This has been a big month for you. It takes you to a time where there is a fork in the road, a decision is required to make the most of an opportunity which is presented to you. This is guiding you to choose a path which is in alignment with your long term goals, this decisive action is a dramatic tool which creates the changes necessary to progress your situation. There is information coming which will help you plan ahead. A surge of artistic inspiration is set to flow into your world. It rules a chapter of improving your options through utilizing creative solutions. As these waves of a potential break upon your shore, you enter a phase of transformation, and this brings some beautiful endeavors to develop. It grows your talents and inspires your mind. This usher in a chapter which is empowering, enchanting, and enticing. This takes you to a new level of potential, it does see a lot of activity ahead, which keeps you on the go. As a bond is deepened, you turn up the heat and discover a very different landscape that surrounds your life. It does trigger a shift forward, changes lead to fast-moving opportunities which create a wellspring of abundance. It sees you are entering a phase which brings information that can help you plan for future growth. It touches on developing your home and social life. A decision ahead draws a wellspring of abundance into your world. It does take you to a time where you can create space to encourage a lighter chapter to shift your focus forward. This is an opportunity to dance with joy and appreciate the blessings which support and nurture your growth.

Dear Stargazer,

I hope you have enjoyed planning your year with the stars utilizing Astrology and Zodiac influences. My zodiac star sign books are released each year which detail a monthly list of astrological events, and a weekly (four weeks to a month) horoscope. You can find me on my Facebook page where you can get personal astrology or intuitive readings.:

https://www.facebook.com/SiaSands

Feedback is welcomed and appreciated.

Many Blessings,

Sia Sands

Printed by Amazon Italia Logistica S.r.l.
Torrazza Piemonte (TO), Italy